salmonpoetry

Praise for Kevin Higgins's Poetry

"His contribution to the development of Irish satire is indisputable... Higgins' poems embody all of the cunning and deviousness of language as it has been manipulated by his many targets... it is clear that Kevin Higgins' voice and the force of his poetic project are gaining in confidence and authority with each new collection."

Philip Coleman

"With backstage guardians in Paul Durcan (see his titles) and Patrick Kavanagh, Kevin Higgins's work has a buoyant spoken immediacy (often taking the form of dramatic monologues), his poems springing out of colloquial address and celebrating the ordinary through a use of quotidian bric-a-brac, which he often pits – with positive effect – against larger (but no more important) forces...Comedy is part of his poetics, and what I especially like in his work is its swiftness of wit, its tone of buoyant contrarianism and jubilant disappointment"

Eamonn Grennan, *The Irish Times*

"It is a profound compliment to the quality of Kevin's writing that you can disagree with the content and yet find yourself still reading on and appreciating the style. You'd have to say that he is one of the lead poets of his generation in Ireland at this stage." Clare Daly TD

"Gil Scott Heron's The Revolution Will Not Be Televised as retold by Victor Meldrew". Phil Brown, *Eyewear*

"Higgins picks apart the human condition, its disappointments and indulgences, with vigour and acumen." Roddy Lumsden

"...good satirical savagery". The Cambridge Introduction to Modern Irish Poetry, 1800-2000

The Ghost in the Lobby
Kevin Higgins

Published in 2014 by
Salmon Poetry
Cliffs of Moher, County Clare, Ireland
Website: www.salmonpoetry.com
Email: info@salmonpoetry.com

ISBN 978-1-908836-65-6

COVER IMAGES: *Kevin O'Shea*
COVER DESIGN & TYPESETTING: *Siobhán Hutson*
Printed in Ireland by Sprint Print

Salmon Poetry gratefully acknowledges the support of The Arts Council

Acknowledgments

Acknowledgments are due to the following magazines, newspapers and anthologies in which versions of some of these poems first appeared:

The Burning Bush 2 online, *Southword, Boyne Berries, The Recorder* (New York), *The Prairie Schooner* (Nebraska), *The Moth, Establishment Magazine* (UK), *Fightback: The Magazine of The International Marxist Tendency, Neo-neocon.com, Eyewear* (the blog), *The Galway Advertiser, Upstart.ie, Irish Left Review, The Irish Times, New Planet Cabaret* (Ed. Dave Lordan, New Island Books), *The Poet's Quest For God* (Ed. Oliver Brennan & Todd Swift, Eyewear Publishing), *ClareDaly.ie*, the Facebook page of Clare Daly T.D., *Mick Wallace.net, The Scaldy Detail, The Chattahoochee Review* (Georgia), *Crannóg, Random Descent* (online), *Watching My Hands at Work: A Festschrift for Adrian Frazier* (Eds. Eva Bourke, Megan Buckley & Louis De Paor, Salmon Poetry), *The Ofi Press Magazine: International Poetry & Fiction from Mexico City, Cordite Poetry Review* (Australia), *We Know What's Up: Facts For Working People* (online), *Led By The Carpenter* (online), *Poeticanet.com* (Greece), *L'Olandese Volante* (Italy), *Washington Square* (New York), *Harry's Place* (online), *ROPES, Natural Bridge* (Missouri), *Skylight 47, This Never Happened II* (Galway University Hospitals Arts Trust), *The SHOp, Dogs Singing – A Tribute Anthology* (Ed. Jessie Lendennie, Salmon Poetry), *The Clifden Anthology 2012* (Ed. Brendan Flynn), *A Menu of Poems 2010* (Galway University Hospitals Arts Trust), *Upstart.ie's General Election Poster Project 2011, Socialist Unity – Politics, Culture Debate: the blog of Andy Newman Prospective Labour Parliamentary Candidate for Chippenham, The Free State Review* (Maryland), *The Raintown Review* (USA), *Verse Daily, Magma* (London), *The Wolf* (London), *Wordlegs.com, Communist Review* (UK), *The Poetry Bus & Leftunity.org* – the website of the Left Unity Party (UK).

Contents

ONE – Tell Me What You Know

TWO – You Not Here

THREE – Considering The Issues

FOUR – You Are What You've Collected

Tell Me What You Know

Know

The day you say you believe in
        the stock market, Jesus
or certain victory for
        Manchester United,
another day awaits, uncircled
        on any calendar. You'll

have just made it back to the island
        of everything
is going to be alright, be busy
        laughing at the universe
through your gleaming new teeth,
        when woken wide to the fact
the cat hasn't come home, or
        the roses you planted
have mysteriously

        died. Staring into
the big fat crack down your life,
        you'll lock your cares
in a soundproof room
        so no one can hear

the screams. Talk to me
        then, when – miles
from anywhere
        you thought you'd be –
you've mislaid your car, your passport
        your mind
and tell me what you know.

Historically Sensible

You knew for a fact, they'd never
allow a pair of mad eyes with a pistol
near the Emperor and his wife;
and when they did, knew
the war would be done
before the Christmas tree went up
in Chichester town square;
and when it wasn't, that the Germans
must be forced to pick up the bill,
so they never did this again.
You knew for a fact, the Tsar
had a special place in the Russian peasant's heart;
and when he hadn't, that the Bolsheviks
wouldn't last five minutes.
And when they did, they were what
you'd been praying for all along.
Hitler was a joke with an Austrian accent
who'd never amount to anything,
and when he did, you knew for a fact
he had no interest in Warsaw, Kiev, Coventry.

You knew when the turbulence
had done its worst, the Shah
would still be sat on his Peacock throne,
looking taller than he actually was. Khomeni?
In five years' time no one
would remember his name.
And that cowboy actor was never
going to win the White House.

The hijackers you envisaged
always landed the plane
and let the passengers go.

Talking Rubbish

The roast potatoes still in play;
already you've denied
the moon landing, told me
George Bush was a good man
badly advised, and declared
the banking crisis
a trick we're playing
on the Chinese.

By the time the *Vienetta* arrives
we're talking toxic waste.
Words that should be sent
to quietly kill fish
at the bottom of the lake,
you're busy arranging into
sentences.

Your weather forecast
is a chicken carcass
plucked from the bottom
of the compost bin,
wrapped in last week's
Mail on Sunday.

Your thoughts on the four thirty
at Pontefract, an oil spill
which could engulf us all.

Your outlook for the economy
enough to send long tails screeching
back down the warm
brown sewer pipe,

and make me want to join
their pattering, dark army
in search of something that smells
more like common sense.

Innocent

Read nothing into the night vision goggles
    I was wearing when they arrested me.
I never met anyone by the name of
    Whittaker Chambers; know nothing about
the boxes of counterfeit dollars found
    in a lock-up garage the record shows
was rented by someone with a name like
    mine. That isn't me behind the ski mask.
I was fifty miles away, having
    tea with the Dalai Lama,
when my friends shot that
    policeman. Someone must have put
that heavy water nuclear reactor
    in the garden shed
when I wasn't looking.
    I just want
to tend my pumpkin patch.

    That isn't me
handing a leather satchel,
    contents, as yet, undetermined,
to Carlos the Jackal, Dusseldorf, 1973.
    And if it is, I didn't know
it was him. I just want to watch the cat wander
    innocent among the dahlias.

Dear Editor

It is not insignificant. Your archives prove,
before God had the balls
to put pen to paper, I was on record both
for and against bank bailouts, global
Jihad, secret World Government, the transport
of the Jews to the East, and the attempt
by the City Council to quietly replace/not
replace the shrubs on the green opposite.
It is not insignificant. I won't name them here,
but we both know of whom I speak,
Dear Editor. No one gives a damn
what's become of the coastal towns
or bothers any more to listen
to the traditional Irish harp, Dear Editor.
Is it just me? You are what I do nights
when I can't phone radio stations
to violently disagree
with what I said last week
about too many/not enough
American/French/Brazilian flags
on buildings that are none of my business,
or women weeing in all night doorways.
We both know of whom I speak.
Dear Editor, I am not insignificant.
I have written to the relevant authorities.
But only when you say my name,
can I be sure I still exist.

On Getting Away With It

End of October. You go
coatless into a specially arranged
coincidence of sunlight.

I leave the house just
as the rain's begun taking itself
far too seriously.

You read mediocre poetry
to a different woman every
morning over breakfast.

My sex life is a door banging
in a house where
no one's lived for years.

Your greatest ambition
achieved; you're the most charismatic
TV repossession man in all

Hounslow; always
have the children thanking you
and laughing at your jokes

as you unplug and carry
Horrid Henry and *Scooby Doo*
down the driveway.

I'm the type who goes out to buy
a lawnmower
and comes back with an electric chair,

which I keep quiet
in the high weeds behind the garden shed,
spend the next ten years afraid

someone will make me
sit on it.

So Ends The Summer Of Our Discontent

Our hearts calm as Clapham High Street
after a night of rioting. Our world
view solid as the Catholic Church
after the latest outbreak of priests
caught in underwear they shouldn't
have been visiting. The shares

that were to have been our pension
continue to cough up blood. Revolution
is a masked woman carrying
the wine she looted - a bottle of red,
a bottle of white - and what looks like
salad dressing. The government

has authorised the use of
plastic bullets
in the event of disputes
about whose turn it is
to put the bins out
next Monday night.

Nightmares are now
what happens
while we're awake.

Inconvenience: A History

When the housing market went further south
    than the East Antarctic Ice Sheet,
my chiropodist climbed Croagh Patrick
    to consider his property portfolio
and never came back down.
The toe nails on my left foot
are not expected to recover.

    My hairdresser abandoned
me for the scalps of Alberta, Canada.
It's been one bad hair month
after another four successive quarters,
    which reminds me of the time
our landscaper, Seamus, got skinned
    alive and driven around
in the passenger seat of a taxi
    by a breakaway UVF faction.
The Rhododendrons were not
    themselves after that.

Tragic, almost, as the night
    the truck pulled up to take
our family tailor, Shmuel,
    to the train and
Birkenau. Trapped in the nightmare
    from which we're all
trying to wriggle free, I went about my
    business as usual
in desperate need of a decent suit.

Leaving The Party

*"It is time for comrade Shachtman to call a halt.
Otherwise the scratch which has already developed
will become gangrene."* LEON TROTSKY, January 1940

Your straight face
all the years you rhymed
'attack' with 'Iraq', your love
of alliteration that's had you repeating
'billionaire bondholders' each day
for the past thousand (and counting),

your friend "misguided,
but one of the good guys"
who knows for a fact the FBI
are trying to control the weather,
that Richard Perle is slowly killing us
with illegally manufactured clouds
his people are putting in the atmosphere.

It all makes me want to step outside
for air. And once there,
to keep walking, determined to be
everything you're not; to become
a war and injustice activist; to go
door to door campaigning for
social exclusion. To be away,

now, to a secret meeting
at the Israeli Embassy
at the end of which I'll receive
an enormous fee. To have
my enemies dealt with for money
by the security services
of friendly third countries. So
when I wake at three fifty two a.m.
and everything is wrong, I'll know
at least I'm no longer you.

Whereabouts

for Juliet Poyntz (1886-1937)

You deliver envelopes
you must under no circumstances open
to men whose names you never ask
in hotel lobbies in Baltimore, Copenhagen,
Shanghai... No one you know has seen
you in three years. On a New York street

you happen upon an old friend, you used to
like to disagree with – on
big opinioned, diner nights
you can't quite forget – talk over
your newfound
disgust: the white walled cells
into which you've seen people
you call 'comrade' one by one vanish
to be kept awake all night
and confess
under extreme electric light. Over coffee
you are full of
the book you're planning to write.

Already evening. Earlier today,
at a chateau in central France,
Edward married Mrs Simpson.
You leave your room at
353 West 57th Street
to buy *The New York Times*
or some *Lucky Strike*
cigarettes. No luggage
nor extra clothes. Behind you,
everything you own.
A solitary candle
still burning.

Buried in the upstate woods
or smuggled aboard a tanker bound for
Archangel, Leningrad, Vladivostok...

My Inner Conspiracy Theorist

Doesn't believe his own birth cert is genuine,
finds Charlie Sheen's most recent
speech from the balcony strangely
plausible; knows – the way all those Israelis knew
not to come into work that day – that swine flu
was manufactured in a laboratory funded
by Donald Rumsfeld, today's weather forecast
is a wicked lie, the dandelions exploding
up through his otherwise well kept lawn
were planted there by government agents
who lurk in the shrubbery at night,
that the Department of Agriculture laces
the sheep dip with weapons-grade
plutonium to hide the fact
he himself is actually
dead, assassinated years ago
by US special forces
during an otherwise enjoyable meal
in a Chinese restaurant
no one wants to talk about.

Alternative History: Constance Markievicz Gets A Sex Change

for Rhona McCord

"97 years ago people lost their lives in that park over there.
Constant Markievicz gave up his life to enable us to
eradicate suppression, taxation, addiction, criminality..."
TOM D'ARCY of Direct Democracy Ireland

Truth is, Joe, I have it on good authority
that fella Constant Markievicz was shot
by the British in the park across the road.
Secretly buried on the moon by people
with names that, to me, sound
homosexual. While I have you, that man
on the ventilator in Johannesburg
isn't Nelson Mandela but an imposter
installed by the same shower who want
to bring euthanasia to Ireland.

We've reached the stage, Joe, in this country,
which fellas like Constant Markievicz fought
and died over, if a man has the audacity
to tell the people what's really going on,
or even what's not, Special Branch
take daily cum-shots of his Facebook page
and file them away for later use.
Get the Minister on here, Joe.
And when he denies it, you'll know
the truth I speak.

Workshop Laws

Your poems must be devoid
        of cacophony, hope,
shards, love and anything
        that could be described as
mellifluous. You will wage war on
        'and'. Participles will be rarer
than dry Irish Augusts;
        it will almost always be 'go',
hardly ever 'going'. 'But'
        and its best friend 'then'
will be interrogated
        severely at every checkpoint,
only allowed through
        if they don't give
the game away. Excessive
        use of the hyphen must be
ruthlessly rooted out. Whatever
        you compare her to,
let it not be a summer's day. However
        bad the crisis gets,
never go in search of a word
        that rhymes with
bankers. Now
        it's been discovered,
the God particle
        is the new tsunami,
and like every daytime
        radio commonplace,
no longer acceptable.

        Never say: "I'm sad."
Show us the wallpaper
        in the room where
you thought about
        ending it.

To That Imagined Place

Go.
Where you can be sure
the mincemeat contains
no per cent mule;

where you'll not find
even one rough white beard rattling
coins in a stolen milk jug
outside what was once
the adult cinema;

where we'll knit for the world
a new ozone layer;
where 'cancer', 'malnutrition',
'hatred' will be ripped
from the dictionary. There,

look into the gelid eyeballs of the boy
man who puts the mash
into machinations
and never forgets a name,

who doesn't believe in god
because he's convinced
he's him.

A Letter God Should Be Afraid To Open

after Nanci Griffith

I have read your application with interest.
From your astronaut distance
the world may look blue and green. Yes.
The five wide oceans and Himalayas,
you spent Tuesday and Wednesday
perfecting, cannot but impress.

Down here, all my worst things line up
at the end of the driveway, like salesmen
in suits that died years ago,
and begin their approach.

Idiocy rings the doorbell.
The tongue flapping around in his head
enhanced by the slight smell of *Jeyes Fluid*.
I ask to speak to his supervisor,
but the number he writes down for me
is my own.

Unintended consequences
let themselves in the side door,
patio window unnoticed.
The house fills up with
outcomes no one wanted
and no insurance policy can fix.

From here the world is mostly
old clothes, damp bath mats. Death
is at the kitchen table
and tells me: *whatever happens,
it's the same dark place I'm going to
and I won't meet anybody there.*

Thank you for your interest.
But even if you existed,
You wouldn't be up to the job.
       Yours etc.

Remembering the Nineties

after Donald Davie

Our hair got smaller and the TV went on
forever. We waited
for The Stone Roses' second album, or watched
Party of Five. In Washington,
committees gathered to frown
at what had gone on in the President's trousers.

Northern Ireland paused for
what would eventually become
a fully formed thought. Rwanda
was a machete with names on it,
that sounded nothing like ours.
We protested French nuclear testing by
sampling South African white
wine's new found innocence.

Osama bin Laden was a rumour
no one believed and Saddam Hussein
an occasional burst of stomach acid
up the oesophagus. We could board planes
without anyone having to see us naked
through a machine first, and made our No
to apathy heard by not bothering to vote.

While we planned trips to places
we couldn't yet pronounce, politicians bickered
about the Romanians begging on Shop Street.

History was in the bathroom,
putting on her new face.

Ostalgie

for Helena Sheehan

I remember Bertolt Brecht and Red Westerns
in which the Indians were the good guys.

I remember drinking Vita Cola at the University of Leipzig
and Kindergarten kids visiting the factory.

I remember white Trabants with hacking exhaust pipes
and the songs we sang at the World Festival of Youth.

I remember Spreewald pickles
and no beggars ever along Karl-Marx-Allee.

I remember the eyes
of a Felix Dzerzhinsky Regiment Guard
scanning a whole street between blinks.

I remember a place to live
and a hospital that didn't
snatch cents from sick mens' pockets.

I remember rock bands singing in German only;
the lyrics of Wolfgang Tilgner.

I remember no one
unemployed and holidays in Moscow
and Prague.

I remember desks full of schoolchildren
who didn't appear to mind
having to learn Russian.

I remember the man at the next table
listening in on our conversation,
but not as closely as you thought he was.

I remember corpses left on the wire at the Wall,
but only every so often.

The Opposite of Nostalgic

He took against
black and white photographs
and went on to reject
the present: the small ecstasies
of broadband bills paid on time, plants
re-potted as they should be.
Preferred to wallow
in the future:
to hang his hopes on
ideas no one has yet had
while wearing trousers
from the year twenty seventy five,
to write himself prescriptions
for medicines uninvented
in an alphabet
that will be all the rage
a thousand years from now, to sit
in the corner of the room
singing songs that haven't yet been written
about a country we'll one day discover.

You Not Here

Empress of Chickens

for my grandmother, May Maloney (1912-89)

You're two months old. Already
the world's largest passenger ship sleeps
on the ocean floor. Your eyes
are their final blue declaration.
The future plump with war
and gunmen in the kitchen;
you chase then feed
the chickens. Twenty eggs
and you're rich. The shopkeeper's verdict:
"nineteen, my child, nineteen." At seventeen
your New York dreams
are the ship that will not sink but carry you
to *Ah, the summer of 1929!*
When all the world is suntanned.

Four years on, the radio heavy
with Roosevelt and Hitler, you skip back down
the untarred road that's barely a road
with dangerously short hair and news
of the man who, it turns out,
is the wrong sort of rich. Love
is the diamond ring
which has to be sent back;
the box of pretty envelopes
you'll never open again.

You'll be Empress
of chickens; tie the knot
with the man at the bottom of the hill;
trade your brief cigarette holder
for the five decade long
white enamel ceremony
of the chamber pot.
Ten children emerge in single file

into that screaming back room.
Love was the diamond ring
            which had to be sent back;
the box of pretty envelopes
            you never opened again. Your anger,
the shotgun that never went off.

You punished us with holy pictures
and no running water for the sin
            you didn't commit;
each morning measured
            the thatched cottage
you were against the mansion
            you might have been.

Couple In Search Of Script

The man with the complete set
of permanently mislaid
false teeth, to be found avoiding him
under the pillow or on the dark sea bed
of that mug of what
used to be water.

The woman who'll miss
her own funeral, waiting in
for first the plumber
then the electrician.

The man to whom everything comes
labelled 'cheap' and
'over the internet'; who
last time he counted
had one hundred and fifty two
pairs of the wrong size shoes.

The woman who watches the garden grow
crowded with water features
that never worked,
but were great in theory,
like Irish unity, or him

putting everything they have
into bank shares and when it's gone
getting the builders in
to dismantle the house, all three storeys,
because there are no TV melodramas
about those who left well enough alone.

The woman who'll spend
her final hours in a room he had
demolished years ago,
offering herself the sign of peace,
and having her hand
constantly slapped away.

The Voice That Once Rid My World Of Custard

I am not yet three years old
in a country on the verge of Edward Heath;
she's pushing me up
what must be Burnt Oak Broadway. Her voice
my News at Ten, my shipping forecast,
my quarterly report from the Governor
of the Bank of England. All
I have to go on.

I am six years old, don't
want custard anywhere near my slice
of school dinner apple pie. She tells teacher.
From that day on custard keeps
its yellow sliminess to itself. Her voice sweeps
about the place ridding my world
of custard and other lesser evils.

I am twenty, thirty, forty something.
A same but different voice
catastrophic down a telephone line
before nine o'clock in the morning,
announcing the end of the world
because that's when
the world ends.

It is yesterday morning.
I've heard it all before. But now
the wolf has come;
as I speak, is eating her left lung;
and she has no other song to sing. Soon
the others will invade by land, sea and air
with their big saints' faces, their flapping hands
and exclamation marks; make me look

like a concentration camp guard
with my things to do list
for the woman who once
swept about the place ridding
my world of custard
and other lesser evils. To whom
the wolf has come.

That Which Must Not Be Examined

The doctor says: it's all in her head.
But she's not going there.
She won't be reduced to angry
tears by some soft voice asking
"And how did that make you feel?"
The world can blow its nose
on the box of tissues
it has in mind for her.
There will be no couch.

Instead, she lights a fat black candle
to the God of just getting on with it.
Her hates harden into something
no talk can dismantle.
Always the hangover,
never the night before.

She visits every Summer,
stalks about the place snapping
windows shut. You put the kettle on.
She plants suspect devices
all around your sitting room. Awkward
with your tea cup and "how
have things been with you?",
you wonder what shrapnel
will get you
where this time.

The Outlook

Tomorrow will be blustery, easterly
and white; the cupboard bitter
and the trees bare but for
the grey backed crow
you'll have for dinner
if it doesn't take your
eyeballs first.

Tomorrow, though no one asked them to,
snowflakes will again
fasten themselves to the ground
like grief.

Against Togetherness

for Kevin McLoughlin, Kieran Allen and friends
on the occasion of their temporary political marriage

Tolerable
to meet one of them
in an elevator and make polite
meaningless eye contact
on your way
to not the same floor; okay
to make miniscule
talk with one
about promised weather
(which, of course, he's against)
as you sit either side of
the giant pink lampshade
in the brothel waiting room.

But gather them together in conference
or for Christmas dinner, they become
devils with a theory grown
in a rancid tea cup; devils
each with a photo
of his or her own private Kronstadt
massacre of the inconvenient
in their hip pockets; devils
who roll 'poverty',
'debt' and 'future generations'
around on their tongues
like boiled sweets.

They demand the truth
so they can put it in a jar
and spend their whole lives
avoiding it; devils I'll make no pact with,
though the country's begging for change
with a small foam cup
and the cancer's in five different places.

November, 2010.

Not

You not here
to not know what
key goes in what lock;
to tell not exactly the truth
about who said what to whom;
to spend the whole first day
of the January sales
examining tea towels
you end up not buying; to notice
I've not yet mowed the lawn,
to not know when
the oil will run out, or have
a plan B, or a good word
for your enemies; to send me out
at four in the morning in search of
cigarettes; to stand smoking
by the kitchen window and say
this didn't happen; to smirk
and tell the world
moving furniture was never his thing
the day I do my shoulder in
carrying your coffin.

Our Downstairs Landlady's Request To My Mother, London NW 7, 1969

If you're passing the Co-Op please bring me:
a small grapefruit and something for a sore foot;

The *Daily Express* and a rusty forceps;
a box of *Brillo* pads and the cheapest

dentist's drill they have; as many dried prunes
as you can manage and a pair of support tights

with a hole blown in them; a nose hair scissors
and half a jar beetroot; one kipper

and a lorry load of toilet roll.
A gallon of weed killer and bag of kidney stones.

One tin of fish paste and botulism
soup. A comic book for your boy

which, when I give it him, I'll say is something
you could never afford. A personality even

more disgusting than mine, which you'll find
between the meat pies and stuff

for unclogging drains. If you're passing the Co-Op
which you must if you want to get back here

from where you're going. I'll pay you Friday,
when I collect my pension. Remind me.

Calmly and Reasonably

His words appropriate as after dinner mints
tempered with Hydrogen Cyanide. He trusts
you won't overreact
when he tells you his plan
to demolish your house.
The wrecking ball arrives at dawn.
He feels a headache coming on
and doesn't know what's
wrong with you.

To save money which, unlike you,
he understands, the streetlights
in those parts of his brain
marked 'God', 'History'
and 'fancy ideas' remain
turned off.

His idea of a great time
a Saturday night spent searching
for a communal launderette
in downtown Pyongyang.

Along the way everyone telling him:
there is no such place.

Ceremonies I Stand Upon

When you need someone to recite your lines to,
I'll have somewhere else
I have to be. But when, crossing the road
on your way to the Oscars,
you're knocked into a coma
by a passing fire truck,
I'll be happy
to accept the award
on your behalf.

When it's door-to-door war
and your pistol's all
out of ammunition, I'll be
anywhere else
but will organise and march
in your victory parade
on a strong white horse.

When you're sneaking a ghost cigarette
in the kitchen, your last weekend
on Earth, and the belt
of your dressing gown brings
the clothes horse crushing
down on you, I'll leave it to others
to help you into a kitchen chair
and balm your beautiful wounds
but will make sure they pay
for the big fat gravestone
I have in mind for you.

I will be nowhere
'til the commentator says,
"They think it's all over.
It is now!" and the photographer's
on his way.

I Love You Less

Than the suggestion of dead mice
between the floorboards
that perfumes this room you left me in;
less than the disinterred bones
of Malcolm Muggeridge which
I keep upstairs in the wardrobe.
Than the black growing
under what were once my toenails;
or the note uncle Paddy didn't write
before he hung himself.
Than the thought of you
putting down the phone
the day you called work
to wish me happy birthday
and a foreign accent told you
I'd been fired months ago;
I love you less even than that.

Skyscrapers

for John Joe Fahy

Born when the world was busy with other things
and the fields full of cattle
that couldn't be sold. You went away
to build skyscrapers; watched
their steel skeletons go up
on days of infinite, white sunshine;
poured however many thousand
tons of concrete. Each morning
was its own symphony
of machinery and shouting,
written by you.

For two years you shouted
at the tumour fattening
itself on your lung, until
one afternoon it declared
the conversation over. The cough
that never went away became
the bed you never got out of.

The Wednesday before you left us:
seventy six candles and a white
Calvin Klein shirt,
which someone else will wear,
for the man who built
skyscrapers.

Your Things To Do List

Batteries for your flash-lamp, leave
the key in the door like a question mark
as the animals make their morning noise, leave
a bottle of whiskey someone else will drink

the key in the door like a question mark
easier than spilling cattle feed, leave
a bottle of whiskey someone else will drink
your coat folded on the low wall

easier than spilling cattle feed
where the pigs used to live
your coat folded on the low wall
tie a perfect bowline knot

where the pigs used to live
call a halt to a hundred years
with a perfect bowline knot
to your people being here

call a halt to a hundred years
as the animals make their morning noise, leave
people, being here
batteries for your flash-lamp, leave

in your Wellington boots go out.

Seven Sisters

Tube strike! The night time news
throws up its hands, and shows
a train bound for Seven Sisters.
The union leader argues:
*Staff. Someone there, before
it's too late, when a woman alights
alone at a deserted station
to, perhaps, a waiting
rapist.* Half a life time

too late. The absolute
confidence of your shined shoes
singing along the platform as sky
concedes victory to
November twilight. Fate,
an empty waiting room.
Two men quietly
up behind you, one
with a broken bottle.

Afterwards, their plan
to chuck you on the track
rudely interrupted by a train
to Ponders End. Decades

have not dissolved those minutes spent
in your executioners' hands.
You had to kill
each of us off in our own special way.

And we must be happy
to remain dead, hope
wherever you are
you've erased
that November twilight
from the life to which
we've lost you.

Lie Down

He arrives an hour and a half after
        the stage at Woodstock
has been dismantled, or
        the crowd have already
burnt down the embassy. He read
        in one of those magazines
bought with money borrowed
        from his mother's purse,
that turning up late
        is what the age
of Aquarius is all about. Last breast

        fed the day he turned
twenty. His soon-to-be
        wife came gift wrapped and happy
to work, while he heroically
        fails to complete
the *Irish Times* crossword.
        Secretly okay
with War, starving children
        and Death;
as long as they never

        come tugging his sleeve.
Weekdays, after the lunch time
        bulletin, he turns
the central heating
        up high and celebrates
with an epic lie down
        the years he's surveyed
the surface of the water –
        centimetre squared by
centimetre squared – without once
        having gone for a swim.

Them and You

after Dennis O'Driscoll

They go down to the house boat,
where someone is tuning an acoustic guitar.
You stay home alone in your tent.

They drive gleaming sports cars down
motorways built especially for them.
You stall on the Headford Road roundabout.

They are unruffled
as a table cloth at the Lord Mayor's banquet.
You turn an argument about punctuation into
a murder trial, yourself in the dock,
the judge putting on his black cap.

They get their names in the newspapers.
You count how many times
exactly.

They travel to watch Barcelona play
Real Madrid. Your team gets relegated.

They shake hands with people
you wish you'd been introduced to.

They know their way around the wine list.
You drink lager shandy because you're driving.

They have affairs with dental assistants
in third floor apartments by the docks.
You think of nothing else.

They can brush things off.
You have to know why
you weren't invited.

God Has Put You On Hold

And the world has no room
for the things you cannot forgive
in the hour of ropes and razorblades
the priest stuffs his suitcase

with things you cannot forgive.
All you have left are jokes blacker
than the priest stuffing his suitcase
as the water comes under the living room door

all you have left are jokes blacker
than having to rely on the generosity of the bankrupt
as the water comes under the living room door
you're a child playing with matches

and the generosity of the bankrupt.
In the hour of ropes and razorblades
you're a child playing with matches
and the world has no room.

Desserts

With a markered cardboard sign
that says: *Anywhere Else*
Wife is looking forward
to spending less
time with me;
to being driven through
Temple Bar/Venice/Carrick-on-Shannon
in a rickshaw/gondola/tractor
with the warm wind up her dress.

I tell her my plans
for the immediate include
a pair of red, expandable pants
and all the episodes of *Judge Judy*
I never got to watch. Some time out
to study my theory of the permanent
dressing gown.

Later, before the tide goes out for good
my hair will enter a peroxide phase,
that'll generally be seen
as a mistake,
covered up in the end
by a peaked cap
which, to most, will say,
when I'm found
with my head kicked in
on a random bathroom floor,
that it was nothing I didn't deserve.

Considering The Issues

The Euphemisms

after Peter Reading

A great and sure remedy
for unmarried ladies. A boat
somewhere so she can sort this out
and then get back to her life.
A Ryanair flight to Leeds-Bradford.
A pill the modern woman
can take with her coffee.
An ex-nurse above a fish and chip shop
who helps girls in trouble.
A day trip to a clinic
near Liverpool. Flushing it
down the lavatory. Something
the Irish government is in no rush
to legislate for. What the Bishop of Kerry
is definitely against.
Something no one wants.
The world's second oldest profession.
A number in England her doctor
suggests she phone.
Something the Irish government
will deal with in a prompt
and appropriate manner.
The constitutional amendment of 1983.
The letters A, B, C. The letter X.
If we leave it long enough
all the letters in between.
Something you can't have women
walking in off the street
and demanding.

Alternative Proposals

"the Fine Gael health minister proposes a panel of two obstetricians and four psychiatrists – one of whom must be a perinatal psychiatrist – to assess a woman who is seeking an abortion on the grounds of suicide ideation...there are only three perinatal psychiatrists in the country"

The Sunday Times, April 21st, 2013

Any woman of child bearing hips,
unfortunate enough to find herself
alive on the patch of weeds between Muff
and Kilmuckridge, or Skibbereen
and Hackballs Cross, must,
to have her baby/babies
legally *abhorted*, obtain, before she kills her
self, without bribery or offer of
sexual favours, the signatures
of six former members
of the Irish National Liberation Army;
six personal friends of Shane Ross;
six random guys shouting
obscenities in the street;
six women from Barna
who thought Michael D's speech
last week to the European Parliament
was absolutely marvellous;
six Sean Nós dancers in residence
at accredited universities,
six plumbers who'll definitely be there
first thing Tuesday morning,
six Dutch guys from Doolin
who make their own clogs, or
six ex-members of the pop group
Six.

Irish Government Minister Unveils Monument to Victims of Pro-Life Amendment

On a date to be confirmed,
when those who remember 1983
will sleep safely in their graves,
or be anxiously telling nurse
about the auld ones with crucifixes
they think are coming to get them

a girl, today
on holidays from primary school,
by then grown into
a Maggie Thatcher suit, will thank
the Chamber of Commerce
for use of their microphone
as a pulled chord unwraps
this thing chipped from stone

in memory
of those forced
to change trains at Crewe clutching
solitary suitcases that screamed
one night only,

those that bled out in the backs
of London taxis after journeys
made possible by post office accounts
and extra hours at the newsagent's;

all because of a stick
which, for them, turned
the wrong colour
the wrong year
in the wrong country.

And as the Minister continues,
across the road a little girl will grab
her mother's arm and ask:
what's that lady saying?

What The Virgin At Knock Would Say If She Could Speak

for Breda O'Brien and all at the Iona Institute

We need to get back
to when confirmed bachelors
found their own kind through holes in cubicles
during untelevised All Ireland Finals.
To when there were no government funded
lesbians on display in public parks,
or self-confessed sodomites in the Senate.
To when there was no obscene use for
Vaseline, or sexual intercourse in Headford.

To when no one put Coke bottles
where they weren't supposed to go.
And there were no automatic
washing machines for women to sit on
when Rock Hudson was unavailable.
To when the Irish people stood
at the end of lanes waiting
for nothing to happen,
which it mostly did.

To when young ones who forgot to cross
their legs at the crucial moment could be put
steam ironing curtains for the golf club, sheets
and pillowcases for your mother's B&B;
still be safely there eight o'clock
in the evening having hot flushes
the hottest day of that century
to which we must get back.

Tidings

The white waves brash
open Atlantic. It's Christmas
day in the empty hotel
and I am not here. So
turn the heat off. The bit
of grey sunlight playing by itself
in the lobby is the ghost
of great summers past. I'm the man
who didn't survive
wintertime and the dying
is difficult. Hard work
and hatred. In years to come
old men will gather around
the helipad and dribble on about how
in days of yore helicopters
would land here. Helicopters
in days of yore
dribble on about how
around the helipad
old men will gather hatred
and hard work
difficult is the dying
and wintertime
who didn't survive? I'm the man
of great summers past
the ghost in the lobby
playing by itself
the bit of grey sunlight
turn the heat off
so I am not here
in the empty hotel
it's Christmas day
brash open Atlantic
the white waves.

Austerity Mantra

Everything must be on the table.
Your ninety seven year old granny
	is no longer cost effective, would
benefit greatly from being brought face to face
	with a compassionate baseball bat.
The figures speak for themselves and will
	be worse by morning. The paraplegic
in his insanely expensive wheelchair
	will have to crawl as God intended.
Here are the figures that won't stop
	speaking for themselves, this is the table
everything must be on. Yesterday my name was
	Temporary Fiscal Adjustment.

Tonight, the insect in the radio calls me
	The Inevitable. When the economist
puts his hand up, take care not to cough.
	Everything's on the table and
the table's tiny. I'd send you a pillow
	to hold hard over the child's face
'til the kicking stops, but at current rates
	there'll be no pillow. I am the unthinkable
but you will think me. Pack her mouth
	with tea towels, hold down firmly
your old mildewed raincoat,
	'til there's no more breath.

Tomorrow I'll be known as
Four Year Consolidation Package.
	Lock the cat in the oven and bake
at two hundred degrees centigrade.
	Tie your last plastic bag over
your own head. The figures speak for themselves
	and there is no table.

Regime Change

No more sitting on white window sills
minding our own whiskers.
The age of cat is over. Now comes
the community of dogs.

Sniffing each other's backsides
is the new global greeting. No more
sitting on white window sills. The daily news
a sound only we can hear. We do

all our business in the public park
and don't care who sees us. No more
sitting on white window sills. In the name
of loyalty we go happily after

our master's kill, return
with peacocks between our teeth. Our walks
always someone else's idea. No more
minding our own whiskers
whitely on a window sill
we thought belonged to us,
now the community of dogs
has come.

Use

Now the world's jobless again
and the government's stopped threatening
to buy you an alarm clock, you can safely
get up every afternoon and campaign
for the right to work;
be back by midnight rejigging
the first paragraph
of your novel that's not
exactly a novel.

With your new orange sweater
and the big fat Easter egg you hide
in the cupboard when anyone visits,
you're every auntie's favourite
charity. The skin disease
you've been cultivating
is coming along nicely.

After we last spoke,
I checked my wallet and my soul
and found some part of both
missing. In more innocent times
you'd have gone to the gallows for being
a waste of valuable oxygen
or someone would simply
have set you on fire.
But petrol is expensive
and no one can be arsed
to do the paperwork.

You potter about the epochs, happy
to be everyone else's fault.

You Are The Nation's Conscience Awake

And nothing you do in the bathroom
smells of anything
but Sweet Alisons declaring it
Summer on country lanes.

At the morning mirror
you embellish yourself
with the best possible motives before
climbing into radio and opinion page
to dump sack loads of concern
on innocent espresso drinkers
from Malin Head to Schull.

You make them come to terms
with the victims of everything
and its opposite: those
who, because of this skinny latté
I'm drinking now,
found themselves headless and penniless
and born out of wedlock; the armless,
the hairless, the maladjusted, the meek
on whose behalf
you're inheriting the earth.

Among Aliens

This dole queue speaks no English,
but Brazilian, Polish
and what might be
Ukranian. Last week,
your brother, the blocklayer,
successfully torched
the house the bank took back,
but the new owners were out.
This morning Australia was sorry
to inform you it has no vacancies
for an ex-millionaire maker
of wrought iron gates that can be seen
all over Mayo and Clare. Back here,
a black toddler chews
her father's Social Services Card.
You look at her
and know

this time it won't be columns
of big boots beating out
wrong! wrong! wrong!
as far as Leni Riefenstahl can see;
but the guy with a million hits on Youtube,
his mouth full of euphemisms,
as he leans in to say: *My dear people,*
we must do something,
or cease to exist.

Unbecoming

"In a time when we have struggled with our identity as a nation, we try now for the new." Dani Gill, Welcome to Cúirt 2011

All we became
has left the building:
the annual increase that meant
a Polish cleaner,
or a trip to sample
the bargains of New York;
that we were free to experience
new European beers
and the government could
stay where it was. Nobody cared
what was on page fifty seven
of anybody's manifesto, or told us
"Capitalism's a nice idea,
but it'll never work." Both
God and Karl Marx left us alone
with the higher truth of
our triple A rated financial products.
Our new white mansions made
the countryside a page crowded
with exclamation marks.

Our years these –
and they won't be back this way,
never, now we're conscripted
onto unforgiving back-to-work scheme chairs,
on which we must learn
to be someone else.

Community Employment Scheme

for Jack O'Connor

I am the thin fat man woman
you have been assigned to,
henceforth known as
The Co-ordinator.

Before the afternoon's out
I'll have you counting toilet rolls;
or guarding the traffic cones
that live at the bottom of the canal.

You will say nothing
about the blank cheques
you'll never see me sign.
Play the cards I deal you right,
and I'll have your back
fitted with a hunch. The others will know
you as my lovely assistant. You'll spend
your best years penning post-it notes
to yourself, here in the office
with me. You'll get to drink
on the job and hardly ever turn up
and know nothing
about the blank cheques
you never saw me sign. The rest
will be time in the loo.

Malcontents will be dispatched
to my friend the Independent Mediator.
I'm a social inclusion seminar
in a windowless room
no one leaves;
the thin fat man woman
you have been assigned to,
evermore known as
your Co-ordinator.

Not The Winners' Enclosure

You invite the girl
in the Send *Shell* To Hell t-shirt
around for a bit of Swiss Roll,
but she's busy not
washing her dreadlocks.

You stalk Shop Street and pretend
something is happening; text
an old girlfriend about how
the Financial Regulator says

these cash strapped days more
and more people are considering
oral sex as a cheaper alternative
to dining out.

But she's already eaten.

Cafeteria Studies

He's a lime green corduroy jacket.
She's a herbal tea waiting to happen.
He's the one who puts the enigma
into enigmatic, the yo! into yoghurt.

He's the collected thoughts of Oliver St. John Gogarty.
He'll grow up be horn-rimmed and flown in from Princeton.
But for now, he's a lime green corduroy jacket.
She's a herbal tea waiting to happen.

He's deep as the books Ian Curtis would have written,
if he hadn't hung himself. She's
where an oven-roasted Lamb Blanquette meets
The Depiction of Urban Migrants In Recent Chinese Cinema.
They're the lime green corduroy jacket
and herbal tea just now happening.

Lament For A Latter Day Progressive

after Ernest Hemingway

When he visits his sister in Tucson
    and beholds
the magnitude of the burgers,
    he thinks it a pity
America was ever discovered;
    prefers nut roasts

done on a stove powered
    by fair trade
plutonium; invites
    an asylum seeker
to watch him eat breakfast
    every other Friday, asks himself
what this says about our society in which
    he insists on including you.

He takes pride in his work
    directing a non-profit
that makes socially aware
    pornography for
visually impaired former
    girl child soldiers. Before he left
his last wife, he had the affair
    with his secretary blessed
by a liberation theologist;

    last Saturday, spent
so long reading *The Irish Times*
    he grew a second
backside; emerged
    from the conservatory
emitting the words
    Polar Bears, Tibet,
Venezuela
    with the priestly whisper
of someone laying
    a wreath on his own grave.

Prayer for Future Days

When you'll get an electricity bill and be delighted
someone took the trouble to write.
When you'll leap up and down like a man
with a foetus in a jar and a message from Jesus

delighted someone took the trouble to write.
When you'll be the guy with the limp and the dogs
with a foetus in a jar and a message from Jesus
and cut down nettles that weren't harming anyone

the guy with the limp and the dogs
on a back-to-unemployment scheme
who cuts down nettles that weren't harming anyone
and throws pig's blood at former Prime Ministers

a back-to-unemployment scheme
you'll leap up and down like a man
who throws pig's blood at former Prime Ministers.
You'll get an electricity bill and be delighted

someone took the trouble to write.

Critical Support For The Insects

The Stop the War Coalition passed a resolution recently
saying the resistance should use "any means necessary."
Johann Hari, *The Independent*, January 7th, 2005

Nothing against the dressing gowns smoking
by the main, revolving door;
nor the young men ambulanced here
weekend nights with suspected
broken heads.

But when the guru with no face
and John Lennon glasses, who labelled
the man dragged from his chicken wire cage
to be beheaded over the internet
another broken egg
for the anti-imperialist pancake,
takes time out to shout:
Save Our Health Service,

it makes me want to die
in a cold hospital
with no running water, under
the one remaining fluorescent light
which, when the last doctor flees
for the relative safety of Mogadishu,
will begin to blink madly;

where the only thing
that'll make my trolley move
up and down the corridor
will be the insects.

Amtrak: Washington DC to Huntington, West Virginia

At Union Station hope is a t-shirt on sale
at seventy per cent off. Yesterday,
all the bow-tied barristers gathered
in the Hilton Hotel.

At the end of the street
the man from JP Morgan told Congress
investors prefer trophy real estate:
Manhattan office blocks to houses
for the little people.

Out here, the tuxedo gives way
to the pick up truck. Red winter fields
dotted with cattle that will soon be
hamburgers; demolition yards
full of cars that were once
somebody's dream.

Out here, the taxi drivers are all local
in tiny white towns, each of which
glowers on its mountain side
like a schoolmistress.

Out here, guys
who'd have been happy
to point you in the direction
of the hunting supplies store
if they hadn't got
killed in whatever war.

What It Says About You

That when you could be usefully
putting another stain on your waistcoat
    or staring into the toilet bowl
to ponder the true meaning of
    Armitage Shanks; you're here
talking to a guy from
    nineteen seventy,
whose last great idea
    was a stolen transistor radio
through which he used to receive
    Jimmy Savile's voice.

He doesn't want
    fluoride in his elderflower tea, insists
on sharing with the whole room
    the smell of things that died
in his prisoner-of-conscience beard
    the night police special branch ran
not enough electricity through
    his balls. Into our nostrils

the essence of the Yogi's last nappy;
    as you raise the drink you bought
with an Arts Council grant
    meant for something else
to those like him
    who drank the Kool-Aid
but didn't have the decency to
    die.

Anatomy of a Public Outcry

for Mick Wallace

Those with short, uncommented upon hair
but exquisite tax returns, cannot forgive
you being regularly mistaken
for Jesus, or the lead singer in
Poison.

The ninety eighth caller
to Four FM's *Hour of Complaint*
wants you publicly garrotted in, preferably,
New Ross for allegedly eating risotto
at inappropriate hours of the day.

The little guy, once caught
having a wardrobe malfunction
with a tender and merciful
rent boy, wants your big pink shirt
declared illegal
under the strict new dress code
he spends his afternoons dreaming up.

The Times and *Daily Mail* agree:
when the Irish team concede
that third shattering goal,
or it rains in Mayo
for the fourth consecutive day,
it'll officially
be all your fault.

Dear General Secretary

after Osip Mandlestam

You're the folksinger beard
you spent years trying to grow;
the Afghan jacket you used to wear
on Bank Holiday bus trips to Galway.
But the complete set of Bob Dylan LPs
in the corner of your living room
is not telling the truth.

When you read *Animal Farm*, it's to see
how the pigs did it.
Whatever the Revolution demands;
you are what it will get.
Your loudest supporters,
those just out of nappies, or refugees
from the Central Mental Hospital.

The inconvenient turn up accused
of attempted rape, pilfering funds…
you leave it to others to execute the details.
Anyone who questions the verdict
can take their case to the committee
that never meets.

You sleep soundly, dream
of the portrait that'll decorate
every town centre, every crossroads
from Donegal to Waterford:

that folksinger beard
you spent years trying to grow
finally come to heroic fruition.

Newly Elected Face Makes Maiden Speech

I am an idea someone else had
when they weren't thinking;
a fat bouquet from my mother
who always knew it would come
to something like this;
a ventriloquist's dummy
that hasn't yet said anything.

I have nothing against homosexuals,
but am not in favour of them either.
Now you've told me Ché Guevara
was a Communist and Adolf Eichmann
a very bad man, I'll bear those facts
in mind, when talking about septic tanks,
a subject on which I've loads to contribute.
I'm against nuclear war and the Spanish
Inquisition, except when they actually happen.

The Political Divide

Not the slight adjustment of the set
      every however many years; which
bundle of common sense in suit
      you decide to say yes to
until the next time. But the coming out

      into the open of the war
between those who, exam day,
      remembered and wrote down
what the teacher told them
      and those who escaped
to smoke cigarettes,
      (or at least stood there
seriously considering it) around
      the back of the bike shed.
Those who sang beautifully at Mass
      and those who got diarrhoea
so they didn't have to go.
      Those who were a great example
to the whole class
      and those alone in their bedrooms
who thought about joining
      tiny organisations
whose headquarters were raided by cops
      yesterday. Those who got pregnant
and those who went home
      when they were supposed to.

Those happy, all these years later,
      to watch Sir Cliff sing *Congratulations*
to a crowd of Union Jacks
      and those whose names come to mind
whenever a headline screams:
      Fugitive porn star found.

You Are What
You've Collected

Autobiography

I'm a ground floor room with a window
that will not close. I'm a cot
with a cloud of cigarette smoke
floating over it. I'm the watercress seeds
we planted at school today. I'm the week's
worth of ham sandwiches I left under the desk
last day before the summer holidays,
nineteen seventy seven. I'm one hundred
per cent in a science test once,
six percent in honours maths.
I'm the university degree I don't have.
I'm *Between The Wars* by Billy Bragg
for my eighteenth birthday and Auntie shrieking
over the fence, that I was conceived
out of wedlock. I'm action likely
to bring the Labour Party into disrepute.
I'm in contempt of court and must
apologise before we continue.
I'm fourteen cups of tea a day
most days (with the bag left in)
maybe ten cigarettes
in my whole life. I'm two weeks working
for *The Wall Street Journal.*
I'm yesterday's sausage roll
for breakfast today. I'm everything
I've been accused of
that wasn't true. I'm the things
they never found out about.

Mouth

When a whole cup of coffee goes screaming
into your beleaguered laptop or at
airport security you realise
you've mislaid your passport
and he spit–mutters:
you shouldn't have been born,
don't
take it personally.
He doesn't know
his own mouth. And when he tells you

he'd rather be fisted
by a fat trade unionist
than suffer another syllable
about your friend Mona's
most recent divorce/vaginal
dryness/pecuniary embarrassment;

tell him: *it can be arranged.*
And that, on occasions like
this, to talk with him is to wipe
the tenderest part of your arse
on the angriest nettles in his granny's
ever giving back garden.

You Can Take The Man Out Of Eyre Square But You Can't Take The Eyre Square Out Of The Man

for Susan

His head recognises the reality of *Supermacs*
but his heart still steals sweets from *Woolworths*.
His monologues are every St. Patrick's Day parade
since nineteen seventy four; his private thoughts
filthier than the old Eyre Square jax.

His political views are like Curran's Hotel,
not there anymore, but his words still subversive
as someone putting an orange jumpsuit
on Liam Mellows' statue.

His balances are healthier than the *Bank of Ireland*
and *Permanent TSB*, his mouth bigger
than *The Galway Advertiser*,
but his answer to everything is

Dunnes Stores. His stubble sometimes bristly
as a rough night in Richardson's;
his idea of himself inflated
as The Great Southern Hotel.

His greatest stroke of luck
drums and face painting
the day she stepped out of a car
and thought: 'I could live here'.

When You Came Home This Evening

Love, your hat was a toothpaste top
unscrewed to reveal hair
crazier than your mother.
Your nose was a sick baby Robin
and your knees two creaking floorboards.
Your face was a graveyard
just after the funeral
and your stomach
grumbled like Chernobyl.

You discarded your bra
to let your breasts argue
with each other and stood there
looking like something dragged in
by a very discriminating cat
who, when I find him, I'll thank
with waterfall loads of salmon
and all the ham in Shanghai
for delivering you
to this and no other
door.

No Reflection

Since you left,
    the upstairs toilet
has developed what sounds like
    indigestion.
The cooked chicken
    I bought last night said to say
it's missing you.
    The cockatiel
escaped its cage just now,
    went out the window
shrieking: "I don't know what I want,
    but this isn't it."
The doctor called.
    According to his records,
technically,
    I'm dead.
He told me: "Look in the mirror";
    and when I wasn't there
said if you don't come home
    immediately, I may never
see me again. Hope
    you're enjoying your holiday.

Judgement

That bit of black fluff in the corner
of the sky's blue otherwise
is the beginning of raincoats moving in
from the West to prove
the over optimism of your flip-flops.

That glass of wine you're ordering now
you'll look back on as the start
of the night's disasters.

When you miss the last bus,
all the hostels and bed & breakfasts
will be shut. In this town without taxis
you'll sleep in a burnt out caravan
with a woman with big
rough hands. You'll remember

the exact moment you first saw
that crack moving across the wall,
the day the house falls down.

You cannot afford
that book you'll never read,
that dress you'll never wear,
those lessons in that language
you'll never ever speak.

Look both ways and then don't
cross the road. That donut
could be the death of you.

What would the world be
without me here to know this?

Chairman, Galway West Labour Youth, April 5th, 1984

after a photograph by John Cunningham

The future is the thin pale youth
staring definitely into the camera. Hours
shy of his seventeenth birthday. After
the main speaker concludes,

he'll play with his biro and ask
if anyone has any
questions. He no longer follows
the football results quite

as closely as he used to, couldn't tell you
who's on *Top Of The Pops*
this evening, but knows he's for a
socialist South Africa,

if not what it means
to sit top table with a man
who once shared a cell
with Nelson Mandela.

He hadn't a clue
these decades later his big ideas
would have gotten so little; that the truth
is what sense you can make

of a notebook from twenty years ago,
found at the bottom of a box;
your name

on the attendance list of a meeting
full of people you definitely
never met.

School Days: A Photographic History

The monotony of rows and rows of boys
with worse and better haircuts
broken by the loud black leather
of the visiting Bishop's shoes,
big as Cathedrals. The sellotaped
canes everybody knew
Mr X kept in that desk. Behind

the up against the wall
class of nineteen fifty five,
the intact glass of the window
we'd smash at the fag end of the seventies
with an over-ambitious ball.

But under that remembered sky
dull as the national anthem or
the 1916 Proclamation being read
at morning assembly, progress wasn't
us going on to smash them all.

Instead a procession of retiring Brothers
each in his turn being presented
with the requisite colour TV;
and then rows of other boys
with worse and better haircuts
who need know nothing now of the joy
of Brother Virgilius's fist
meeting a bully's jaw.

Trafalgar Square, March

For what you want
abolished: hours of broken glass
and ice cream cones; horses' hooves
hammering hot tarmac. The worst
best riot in history. For one day
becoming night only, you're bigger
than the suffragettes or Nelson Mandela
and will not tolerate
people in expensive cars.
Something has to give
and you think you know
its name. Today,

the day that'll grow up
to be a photograph of a chair
suspended in mid-air;
your life this never ending
grope in the dark,
which when you look closely
is no groping just the dark.
Years from now you'll bring
the woman whose name
you don't yet know here
in similar sunshine to propose
and tell her, that building there
was on fire.

Facebook Ghost

With her not quite beehive she missed
the rock star bus waiting
for her mother to get off the couch.
She was the Hell you went
grinning down into.

You were convenient,
inconvenient.
She was a car bomb. You
just happened to be passing
the Hell you went grinning
down into.

Her words were shrapnel:
wolf, wife-beater, paedophile
and everywhere, before
she tried to take them back.

This morning she ghosts
up out of the computer,
has children now and wants
to be your Friend after
sixteen years and seventeen days –

a dream broken only by
the here and now of Love
opening the window to help
the cat in or out.

The Death of Baroness Thatcher

after Patricia McGuigan and Alexander Pope

Her hair was a headmistress dreaming
of again being allowed to use the cane.

Her ambition was a brass door knocker
on what was once a council house.

Her brain was a conversation about money
Sir Keith Joseph had with himself.

Her back passage was Basil Fawlty
complaining about car strikes to the Major.

The look in her eyes was a shoot to kill policy
in Northern Ireland.

Her sentimentality was a spinster's thimble
in which you could fit what's left of the Tory Party
in Scotland, Liverpool, Manchester,
Leeds, Sheffield, Newcastle...

Her clenched fist was a skinhead
in nothing but Union Jack y-fronts.

She said the word 'Europe'
like a woman coming down
from a severe overdose of Brussels Sprouts.

Her Christmases were dinner at Chequers
with a recently deceased sex offender.

Her 'out', 'no', 'never'
were striking print workers
being given the cat of nine tails.

Her fingers and thumbs
were ten riot shields in a row.

Her final nightmare
was the silent, black eyed ghosts
of Joe Green and David Jones,
who did nothing but each offer her
a hand.

David Gareth Jones, from Wakefield, died amid violent scenes
outside Ollerton colliery in Nottinghamshire on 15 March 1984.
On 15 June Joe Green was crushed to death by a lorry while
picketing in Ferrybridge, West Yorkshire.

Memoirs Of A Carrier Bag

for David Conway

I'm a receipt for fifty pence worth of hummus,
    a small brown Hovis. Tescos.
Edmonton Green. January third.
    Nineteen ninety one.
I'm a return ticket to
    railings being thrown
at the police. I'm the sticker
    the British National Party
stuck on the kitchen window.
    I'm a small, black notebook
full of phone numbers it would now
    be wrong to ever ring.
I'm a piece of orange peel
    from the night the first Gulf War began.
I'm the Deputy Leader of the Council
    in a worn copy of
The Enfield Advertiser stating
    he takes no notice of what
the egregious Mr Higgins says.
    I'm a leaflet, a copy of which
lives in the Enfield Peoples' Museum.
    I'm a pamphlet no one read
about a world that never was.

Prayer For A Friend

for Clare

The past's something by Billy Bragg
on a tape which later unravelled, or
retired to the under stairs home for
hoovers that never exactly worked.

Us all with our coats on
in a house without heat some February
no one but me remembers.
Your mother wondering who

the hell I was that Sunday
she came to visit; you certain
I togged out for the other side. Today is
you still sitting in front of armoured cars

others aren't big enough to resist.
All you wanted come true, so
don't be the girl who died
of her name on the front pages beside

the worst picture they could find.
Though there'll be days miserable as Morrissey,
when hacks with notebooks will go through your bins,
looking like something less

than badly paid secret policemen. Give
not one sour cream and onion flavoured Pringle
for things written by a man with a funny shaped
head in the wrong part of the *Daily Express.*

Camp Rules

By all means explore what remains of the world
on the other side of the forest.
But be back within the perimeter fence
by breakfast, your mouth motorised
by where they're going wrong, or we'll begin
making a sad sound when we say your name,
and tilting our heads slightly to the left.

Questions are encouraged if the answer's
the long form version of 'yes'. Discipline
will be maintained by Nullifier Boyd's
righteous bamboo stick, so big
it never need prove its existence.

Here, no one evades their taxes
or mentions the unfortunate business
you witnessed in the main marquee
this morning. Out there, the last thing
many women notice is that the man
strangling them is in desperate need
of a dentist.

In the new society we're building
we've abolished rape and murder.
We permit no such words.

To A *Smarties* Mug

Bastard child of an Easter egg gone
long into the bloodstream
of someone who's since seen
a doctor's lips shape:
possible diabetes.

Before I got you, abandoned
in that bottom cupboard, beside
the worst kitchen sink in Tottenham
you'd skulked there years minding
your own fungi.

Minutes from the rage that left
P.C. Keith Blakelock
macheted on the concrete;
you knew not a thing
when a woman with a bump, destined
to be Adele and the song
for a future *James Bond*,
padded a nearby street.

Most of a life you've travelled with me,
as the gobs that slurped from you
sundered into factions. Our
loud hopes become cigarette butts
passed out on bus station floors:
Enfield, Croydon,
Portsmouth, where I cradle you now
September evenings and know

end of story
this is not.

For Darrell On The Occasion Of His Fiftieth Birthday

At thirty, you were Tottenham's premier
bingo calling Trotskyist,
centrefold of choice for old women named Ethel
who liked a bit of clever,
all set to become a creepy
old man of questionable sobriety
who takes tourists on horse drawn
treks around the less interesting bits
of Dewsbury, West Yorkshire.

Tonight, we raise tumblers brimming
with something excellently French
to your metamorphosis into
the potential owner of a boat,
to ideology gone soft as butter
left hot weeks in the boot of the car,
to the hope Wednesday
won't be as bad as they're saying.
The only thing bothering the Dordogne sky:
where on your tea stained atlas of France
to invest the fat tens of thousands
you haven't put by.

You Dream Again of Bus Conductors

In that corner of your mind
that's always on its way into Leicester, circa 1979.
Men in brown coats deliver rented TVs.
Your sister's going out with an arsehole called Andy,
and smoking is good for you. You gobble
nationalised sandwiches on trains
that are all the same colour. These are the years
of porridge and brick built buildings before
automatic doors made us all soft. A simple
painted sign with the name of the owner
sits above every shop door. The air is the exhaust
fumes from the local factory. Sunday
is nothing open and nobody phoning.
Looking for the future,
you join The Labour Party
and find the past.

But there's always someone to punch
a proper hole in your ticket
and tell you where to get off the bus.

To Avoid Disappointment

Know there's more to life, lad,
(and so much less) than disco dancing
and driving around France
only to find it closed;

than students being for and against everything
nights you know what you're saying,
though tomorrow you'll have no idea
what it was. Somewhere else

snow waits for soldiers
to drive their big boots
through it. Dogs, barbed wire
and security checks begin to cohere

against the soon to be huddle
of prisoners, who'll be led away
to their own statistical
inconsequence, but who
this morning wake

in rooms free and ordinary as yours
to exam and pregnancy
test results softened by
mugs of unsweetened tea.

Leather Intellectual

Of a winter, summer
or in between evening
down pub, instead of Dominos
he preferred a nice game of
Marxism. His favourite word:
'outrageous' said
in the not posh London accent
he had updated annually.
So fixed on the bigger picture
he didn't know
up from down. Geezer
to whom nothing human was etcetera,
except bastards who roll
their own cigarettes. His contribution
to the international working class movement
useful as what his favourite
heavy metal band used to
leave behind them in the hotel room.
Great in theory. In practice
they couldn't tell
if he was alive or dead.

Being Vladimir Ilyich

for Gerry Matthews who recruited 'the Irish Lenin' to politics

He sweeps the driveway Sundays,
    names each fallen leaf
'god', 'capitalism' or 'monarchy';
    then indoors to count the raindrops
on the window pane and wait
    for World War Three.

He lifts the toilet seat and asks himself
    what would Vladimir Ilyich do next?

He harangues wide faced students
    with words borrowed from a book,
the first page of which
    he's actually read.

He supports every striker's cause,
    as twine supports corpses
strung from trees. Delighted
    to be losing his hair, each morning
he's a few per cent more
    Vladimir Ilyich. Devastated

no one's yet sent him
    a letter bomb or flavoured
his apple tart with Arsenic.
    He speaks hours
on the need to weed out dogmatists,
    functionaries, feminists...
He's grown the Party from a phone box
    to a decently sized school hall.

Tomorrow, he'll put it back in the only
    phone box in town
not yet torn down.

You Are The Old Man In The Blue House

after Bertrand M Patenaude

Making impossible promises to yourself.
Outdoors the cactus, the wolves.
The hour of nowhere else to go.
It's a decade since the new god stamped
your passport 'invalid'.

Your fifty-ninth birthday is candied plums
and two small orchestras.
Out there your friends welcome
bullets in the back of the head.

An August storm batters the porch
with the Chief Prosecutor's words:
Down with the vulture, these miserable hybrids
of foxes and pigs!

In your hand
the pistol with not enough ammunition.
You wait for you know not who
to hug your skull and whisper.
"Everything is finished";

indulge in just one more
promise that won't come true over
the candied plums and two small orchestras
in the hour of nowhere else to go.

The Man Who Put The Laissez
Into Laissez Faire

I went looking for the inevitable
so I could spend a lifetime bowing to it.
I wasn't arrested for espionage
during the Spanish Civil War. That man
standing in front of the tank
definitely isn't me. I don't
dare open a door for fear
I might have to go through it.

My ambition now
to be mistaken in the coffee shop
for a former child star
who these days makes records
no one even bothers to reach over
and turn off; to look like
I could have been
the background music
for a dinner date that didn't happen
because of his rampant alopecia,
her bad knee
in a restaurant they eventually
decided not to build.

Crowbar

She jiggles her one year old on her knee
and smiles like Magda Goebbels,
of whom she has never heard.
If you don't have central heating,
more fool you for having no respect
for yourself. She is not au fait
with trade unions. Her laughter,
a bag of rattling crowbars
and always at someone else's
expense. *If you didn't get paid*
no one to blame
but yourself. Her husband's income
bracket, no one's business
but hers and the guy she shares
occasional hotel rooms with
in Limerick and Ballybofey.
Her chin, you could skin
several cats with. *No such thing*
as poverty in Ireland today,
as anyone who's ever had
a proper job would know.

One stray word and she'll put
child pornography
she had specially made for you
in your office drawer;
but you know, in a flash,
she'd be down on her knees
if she thought some temporary advantage
was to be had in your pants.

Each of her days its own picket line
she pleasures herself by crossing.
She is not au fait
with trade unions but smiles
like Magda Goebbels,
of whom she has never heard.

Blue

When the whiskey doesn't work
and the dog makes off with your dentures.
When your stomach's a volcano
that won't just shut the fuck up.
The crack down the side of the house
opens its mouth and laughs.

When there is no milk
and that yeast infection's back
and you forgot to turn on the oven
and the suppositories go horribly wrong.
The crack down the side of the house
opens its mouth and laughs.

When it's raining giant ice golf balls
on your roses, and that mug of black tea
hits your new tan pants like the Exxon Valdez.
The crack down the side of the house
opens its mouth and laughs.

When the doorknob comes off
in your prosthetic right hand,
and your granddad's coffin won't close.
The crack down the side of the house
opens its mouth and laughs, as if
you're the joke it's telling itself.

Plagued

The dachshund smells something off you.
You've become the bloke
you met twenty winters ago, waiting
for a train that wasn't coming –
with the cough his new inhaler
should've taken care of – you're
desperate to share
that your left pebble
this morning swelled
to the size of an enraged, bulbous
orange.

It's either
the nothing that, if it's anything,
they've caught it in good time;
or the silent, embedded
something that, within six months,
will zip you up and drive you
around the roundabout
in a bag to be discarded. Money

for next year no longer the worry.
You've enough in the drawer,
that's been too crammed to close
for years, to pick up the bill
and tip the driver
nicely.

The Necessary Arrangements

Write it all down, she says, on the back
of a Tax Clearance Cert, or one
of those dead political manifestos
that keep you up all night in the study:

what you want done
when you step out in front
of a terminal 46 bus, or
get your leg caught in a passing
combine harvester; cease to be
anywhere you can give the world
the benefit of your advice.

She says, last time she looked,
most of my parts were in adequate
working order. But it's never too
early to start choosing
a hat for the funeral.

No hat, I tell her, turn up
with a black scarf fastened
to your grief-stricken head. If at all possible
get someone to sponsor the coffin
and every cent you can
from the relatives. Put
my dentures and other
detachable bits immediately
up for auction. Employ

a church load of Anglicans
to tell lovely lies about what I was like;
a choir to sing *Holiday In Cambodia*
as I'm rolled out the door. Poets
who shuffle up sheepish

demanding a microphone
from which to sing my praises
should be buried with me
and never spoken of again.

If the city fathers
name anything after me,
make sure it's a block of flats
with Thatcherite hallways
where skinny dogs can disagree
to their hearts' discontent,
and sellers of socialist newspapers
not yet born
can tell children with cigarettes
and guys in boxer shorts they got
free with *The News of The World*,
about the working class and how
they have nothing to lose
but their tracksuit bottoms.

Apart from that, do
whatever you think appropriate.

KEVIN HIGGINS facilitates poetry workshops at Galway Arts Centre and teaches creative writing at Galway Technical Institute. He is also Writer-in-Residence at Merlin Park Hospital and the poetry critic of the *Galway Advertiser*. He was a founding co-editor of *The Burning Bush* literary magazine and is co-organiser of Over The Edge literary events in Galway City. His first collection of poems *The Boy With No Face* was published by Salmon in February 2005 and was short-listed for the 2006 Strong Award. His second collection, *Time Gentlemen, Please*, was published in March 2008 by Salmon. His work also features in the generation defining anthology *Identity Parade – New British and Irish Poets* (Ed Roddy Lumsden, Bloodaxe, 2010). *Frightening New Furniture*, his third collection of poems, was published in 2010 by Salmon Poetry. Kevin has read his work at most of the major literary festivals in Ireland and at Arts Council and Culture Ireland supported poetry events in Kansas City, USA (2006), Los Angeles, USA (2007), London, UK (2007), New York, USA (2008), Athens, Greece (2008); St. Louis, USA (2008), Chicago, USA (2009), Denver, USA (2010), Washington D.C (2011), Huntington, West Virginia, USA (2011), Geelong, Australia (2011), Canberra, Australia (2011), St. Louis, USA (2013), Boston, USA (2013) & Amherst, Massachusetts (2013). *Mentioning The War*, a collection of his essays and reviews was published in April 2012 by Salmon. It has been described by Clare Daly TD as "a really good and provocative read. It will jolt you; it will certainly touch you; make you laugh; maybe make you snarl a little bit as well, depending on where you come from or what your background is." Kevin's poems have been translated into Greek, Spanish, Turkish, Italian, Japanese & Portuguese. *The Ghost In The Lobby* is his fourth collection of poetry.